I0187186

Down This Crooked Road

Modern Poetry From The Road Less Traveled

Edited by
RD Armstrong & William Taylor Jr.

© 2009 by RD Armstrong & William Taylor Jr.

All Rights Reserved. No portion of this book may be reproduced without express written permission of the editors, except for purposes of review.

ISBN 978-1-929878-03-1

First edition

Lummox Press
PO Box 5301
San Pedro, CA 90733
www.lummoxpress.com

Printed in the United States of America

Some of these poems have been previously published in these magazines: 2 River View, AntiMuse, Blue Collar Review, Chiron Review, Concrete Meat Press, FIRE, Flashquake, Gnome, Guerilla Poetics Project, Instant Pussy, Lunatic Chameleon, Meat , Naked Knuckle, New York Quarterly, Outsider Writers, Over The Transom, Poems For All, Red Hills Review, Remark, Underground Voices, Word Riot, Words Dance, Zygote in My Coffee, Dogmatika, Coffee House Poetry #6, Broadside #12; A little poetry, Hecale, Forget You Books, Zeitgeist Press, Flashquake, Raw Art Press, Beat Museum , Word Riot, AntiMuse, Kendra Steiner Editions, Sisters of the Page, Rusty Truck...We also apologize to any magazines we may have forgotten to mention.

Down This Crooked Road

Introduction
by William Taylor Jr.

A little while ago Raindog and myself were
throwing around the idea of doing another book
together, and at some point RD, I think, suggested
doing an anthology of sorts. He invited me to so-
licit work from a handful of my favorite poets, and
we'd go from there.

The idea excited me and it didn't take me long to
make a list in my head of the writers I wanted to
include. They pretty much came to me right away.
Not only are the writers collected in this anthology
all wonderful poets whose work deserves a large
audience, there is something about their collective
work that seems to especially shine when gathered
together in a single volume.

The poets included here are not from a particular
school, at least not one that has been invented as
of yet. They don't all hail from a particular region,
though RD did point out that none of them are from
Los Angeles, which means something in the world
of Lummox. For those keeping score, four of the
poets (including myself) live in California, two
from more eastern regions of the U.S. and we have
the lone Miles J. Bell from the UK.

What connects these writers in my mind is obviously not location, or even style of writing, but more a spirit that I feel shines through in the work of all involved. All the poetry contained here is accessible without being mundane, well crafted without being academic...Poetry for people who might not realize they like poetry.

It is my belief that your average reader can pick up this volume, open it to any page, read a bit, and think: This makes sense to me. *This is a fellow human sharing their vision of what it is to exist, and it inspires me.* Or, it could well be they'll think something more along the lines of: *This is some cool ass shit!* That works too.

In any case, the authors collected here are writing some of the best poetry out there right now, period. I'm excited and honored to have my work appear alongside them. The death of poetry is a silly, vicious little lie, and this volume attests to it.

Table of Contents

M.K. Chavez   11
Love, My Monster of Grace
The Baptism of the Alchemists
A View of the Bay
Colma, California
Everything that I Needed to Know
More Human
Mission Street Love Story
Suicide Poems
Ryden's Girl
Patron Saint of Wayward Girls
Ode to Methamphetamine
Meat Tags
San Quentin Senryu

Christopher Cunningham   29
GO
last meal of the night
the lateness of the hour
horrors of the wet morn
dawn
bending, but not the other
blue mouse
a sure thing
the animals
a song in the night like a laugh
college park, georgia
unguarded
down this crooked road

Miles J. Bell 49

Half-full for me despite my protestations to the contrary
Unlucky
She watches him eat
Love the night
The good and the wise lead quiet lives
Icarus Rex
2 Kinds of Nostalgia

William Taylor Jr. 71

Slow
Christmas at The Brown Jug
Rainy Afternoon
John Berryman, They Say
I Bet They Never
The Heat
Madness
A Truth I Could Only Imagine
A Fool With a Four Dollar Frappachino
The Strangest
The Insect
Mickey's Place
Bad Night
It is Enough

Christopher Robin 97

Saved
On the Assumption of My Usefulness (for Silvi-Ann)
Girls Don't Look
How to Turn an SSI Check into Pimpin'
Freaky Mumbler's Manifesto

Infinite Joy In Spite Of
Slingshot
I Want to Be a Better Asshole
Searching for Joan of Ark in Front of Safeway
Too Much Me
Who We Kill

Father Luke   117
Come Home
It Will Never Be My Turn
Holes in the Shadows
With a Seagull for Company
Purpose
The Contender
Fri3nd
Hi. It's Miguel
Arizona Still Life
Throw a Gun on the Casket
The Path
The Dog Did It
Something Other Than Myself

Hosho McCreesh   134
In Every Place The Sun Drags It's Light,
        & In Every Shadow That Aches For It,
        In Every Single Place That Exists,
        & In Every Single Place We Can Imagine...
In This Our Darkest Night,
        In This Our Age Of Stillness,
        Of No Light, No Insight, No Inertia...
October in America

They're Feeding The Pigeons In Venice,
> *& Someone In Amsterdam, In Paris,*
> *Is Standing In Front Of A*
> *van Gogh*
> *Weeping...*
A Poem For
> *Anyone*
> *Who Cannot*
> *Be*
> *Happy...*
You Never Want To Say That
> *We Owe It To Ourselves*
> *To Be As Happy As We Can Possibly Be*
> *For All The Many & Nefarious Ways It'll Be*
> *Taken Out Of Context, Be Co-Opted*
> *By The Greedy, The Self-Important,*
> *The Gluttonous, & Idiotic & Insatiable...*
One For The People Who Think It's
> *Easy To Write Poems, & For Those Who Think*
> *Poems About Ex-Lovers Actually Matter...*
As Madness Abounds, As Brutality Trumpets, &
> *A Cold, Hard World Gets Colder, Harder, &*
> *The Death Of All That Might Save Us*
> *Increases...*
One for the Bulls,
> *No, One for Us..*
A Majestic 50 Year Old Cottonwood
> *Sick With Some Kind Of Infestation & Rot..*

Bios   152

M. K. Chavez

Love, My Monster of Grace

My Dracula enters the room on his fingertips
there on the small space of wall, space
of air, between our mouths open, with
repetition, like this, this and this, the

exchange. Twang of keys, unlocking, unlocks,
the hinge of empty air, air that we breathe.
Breathe in you and me, the soft ping, ping, ping,
ping of the piano keys, this is art. Light

surrounds the mundane and muted air.
Heart like the train station in Amsterdam
in the winter, even the birds listen to
the ting, ting, ting of time, blind. Time is black,

tender as a moth's wing, your canvass, I
could never write into lines, the iris
open, opens. Bleeds, drip, dripping, life into air.

M. K. Chavez

The Baptism of the Alchemists

I pour the gasoline
You light the match
and we stop
take in the view
a red sky burning
the sun coming
to an end
as we touch.

Our clothes come off
we take pictures

of the skin of the soul.

In the hotel room
we believe in good luck
we believe
that we see
the right path

and then we are lost.
All that we wanted
was a little warmth.

Touching the fire
is too much. There is nothing
like the burn of us.
You touch me
and we disappear
like pale blue smoke.

A View of the Bay

I take him on a walk behind Golden Gate Fields,
    stand him
before the water and the city, make him look at the
    view.
He says there's nothing to see and blames everything,
the elements, the things that we can't control.
I describe the diversity of grayness
and point to the seagulls but he dismisses them as
    plain.
As they pass overhead, I place one hand on his chin
and tilt his head to the sky. I tell him that it takes
    strength
to glide, to hover the way birds do, above us.
I point to individuality, the base of lightness, the span
of the wing, and lineage. I force him to study the
    steadiness
of one simple slate colored gull. His eyes are glassy,
they hold little but a reflection. I don't expect any-
    thing to happen.
I don't expect him to see the miracle
of the scavenger, begging, waiting
for discards, waiting for humans
to be kind or careless.

Colma, California

Call me heart, the final escape.
Sit down and eat air. I like

to share it. Secrets are buried
every day. I hold them like stone.

Come to me after they've killed
the god in you, when all that's left

is white as chalk, cold as marble
and I'll open my wings, keep you

company, blow angel kisses
when no one is looking. Bury
your dead.

Everything that I Needed to Know about Writing I Learned from Being a Stripper

Each no brings you closer to yes
you just have to keep at it.
Sometimes it's the ugliest of moments that brings you
    closer
to the money shot. Beauty is ethereal, you might be
the most beautiful girl to one and a leper to another.
In the audience you will find flat-eyed faces
looking at you like you're deformed
and then you'll find
the lovers of the deformed
and they'll make you god for a few minutes
and that's all any one needs.
I learned that it all adds up.
Words on a napkin become poems, poems on a page
become books. It's something
you can hold in your hand.
And the dollar that the idiot gave you to sit on his lap
disappears into a stack of bills
and it's something
you can hold in your hand.
It all adds up.
Some days are good and you are gold
and other days you're wading through mud
like a starving pig, looking for scraps
and you can't figure out what you're doing
in the cesspool of dead words and men
who come to the club to jack off at 11am but don't
have any money to tip. When you approach

the altar you're hoping for a masterpiece, a hundred
    dollar bill
you might get excited for the twenties
but you'll take the fives. You'll take what you can get.
Somewhere along the line you'll become addicted
to the heat that comes from writing a good poem,
or earning your rent in one night. There aren't many
rules, just remember not to fall in love
with the customers, or your words and if you feel
    exposed
you're doing something right.

More Human

I'm in bed with the wrong man.
The room is painted
an ugly color
we both agree
on that. I shouldn't complain
beggars can't be choosy, I beg
him to stay. He leaves, I stay
he comes back and we're there
again, between white sheets, as if
we are clean, and he tries
to find a way to make me see
things differently. He calls the color
mauve. It sounds better
for a moment. We have to face
facts; the pink carnation colored room
is putrid. I tell him that we can't
do what we're doing, he agrees
and pulls me closer and it's wrong
but it's so human.

Mission Street Love Story

On 16th and Valencia
Christmas lights blink all through the year.
"Esta Noche" looks like my kind of bar. I like my genders
slightly stirred.

Sergio, the outreach worker, calls it "Esta Nightmare,"
and hands out condoms to women who used to be
men, who he'll fuck
after the lights have stopped their garish show.

There is cilantro in the air
and the sweet smell of muscled men
holding hands. I get hungry
watching the brown skinned butches with their femmes.

In the gutter on the corner of 17th and Mission
if you look closely enough
you might see a twenty dollar bill,
a collection of rotting teeth,
a small baggie of sticky yellow cocaine
to shoot along with your black tar. Shards
of green-night train-glass, above it
on the curb is a hooker's pride.
She negotiates a ten dollar trick.
If you look at her too long
she'll kick your ass.

And the school girls on 24th and Guerrero
roll up their skirts before stepping through the arches

of the Church of the Immaculate Conception. One
        of them
is pregnant for sure, and the other one will be soon,
        and neither
of them knows what hell really means, at least
not yet.

There's a new 99 cent store next to the place where
        you can buy rosaries
and first communion dresses, and the taqueria
        that's been there for 25 years
now offers vegan alternatives. You can still buy
        crack on the corner
in front of McDonalds.

Things haven't changed all that much,
you can still get all you need in the Mission,
but now if you want you can have a cute white boy
pierce you and slide a ring through your nipple
while he tells you all about his Prince Albert.
And if you find yourself alone at night you can get
        drunk
with Lesbians at the Lexington,
have your nails done at the Beauty Bar,
eat overpriced tapas at Cha Cha Cha,
pick up a good book or a drunk poet at a used book-
        store,
shoot dope in the bathroom at the Uptown,
get harassed by drunk frat boys, gang bangers
and hipsters all within a one block radius,
and when the pain & the suffering hits

you can bury your dead at Driscolls,
and mourn on the streets,
no one will stop you.

You can go away,
the Mission will always be waiting,
ready to give you something else,
without asking for anything back.

Suicide Poems

Let them be read the way that I wanted to be loved.
Let them sink into the fibers of unbound paper.

Let them haunt the capillaries of each vein.
Let them be ether. Let them be death.

Let them be immortal, let them be porcelain.
Let them be young girls and old men. Let them be
      fleshless,
let them tell lies.

Let my poems be a sparrow traveling
from the facade of Brownstones
to the faded pastels of Victorians.
Let it not matter if anyone believes in the lungs of
      one little bird.

Ryden's Girl

I will bleed during commute hours,
on the buses, on the trains,
while watching movies,
over buttered popcorn
and bon bons, everything melting
together, all leaking

slowly onto the floor. The soles
of my shoes will make sticky noise
when I leave and walk down the street,
picking up good men
for money, bleeding on paper
and white linen.
I'll bleed spirals

when we make love, I'll decorate
strangers.
I'll sit next to you.
Next to you.
Next to you.

And next to you
I'll bleed.
I'll cook dinner, fold laundry
blood flowing and bubbling,
bleed blossoms for fancier functions.
Arrange all of my flowers
for you.

Patron Saint of Wayward Girls

Santa Alicia, saint of oil slicked Mission Street.
Bless us in the taquerias, cantina's, botanica's

in the mortuaries, and at Dianda's Italian bakery
where ballerinas dance on frosted birthday cakes.

Deliver us Santa Alicia, we don't want to cut our feet
on broken glass. Patron saint of the forgotten girls

pin-eyed girls, pregnant girls, and girls in high-heel
      shoes
standing on 18th street. Have pity for us Santa Alicia,

we hear demons speaking to us from bedrooms and
      alley ways.
Pray for us, who have grandfathers, brothers, and
      fathers,

priests, uncles, and strangers who will not let us
leave. Bless our eyes and our tongues. Take us away

give us a chance to numb the pain. Blessed are you
among virgins, for you are the one who got away.

M. K. Chavez

Ode to Methamphetamine

Sweet caterpillar of my affliction
come back you've gone so far away. Can't
beat the predilection, I try again
to use you, but it just isn't the same.
Ah—I float in my dark aquarium,
try to catch for hours, you slippery through
my fingers. Sing, a sweet requiem to
the smell of you, like the burnt synapse,
musk of Benzedrine. *Please.* How I
miss wearing my skinny jeans. I even

love the dreams and the ghosts of my brain.
The curtains and sheets from my modest house
on Sumner Way, tight fit ally off of Market
Street, where I thought everything so discreet,
where I hid and overdid. So much, yes,
I rose above, and when the old man upstairs
outlived death and put his coffin out for
the garbage beat I picked it up, and slept
in it. *Each line God.* I resorted to
getting nude, shivered in the cold, turned

a pretty blue, perfection, curled up like a snail,
diaphanous little brittle shell,
carried home on my back. Spent time at
the club, my body shimmering under
the disco ball, a hundred pieces of cut
glass, how beautiful I was. A red haired
girl bespeckled with electricity. *Oh!*

I miss the hotel huffing, the continuous
snorting, and sensuous cavorting, the
kiss of my blissful libido, sweet speed

aficionado and tweaker. How bleak
the world lolls without you. Delusions
the only grandeur the world offers,
and bring the memory of this use
a razor sharp prayer. How judiciously
the mind misses the soft blur of you,
blast of white euphoria, like to feel
the blight of being, a steady gaze
not too much of anything to bother
the sparks of my mind's burning stars.

Meat Tags

Tears are not the same in different countries.
      Not the same for you & me.
      My first boyfriend still lives
      in San Quentin which is a place
      unto its own. He'll die of Hep C,
      which is a terrain of pummeled meat.

The liver holds anger. You can get bruises
      from carrying something
      that weighs too much.

The petal skin of my inner thigh blossomed
      red & purple after passion
      with him. I was always sad
      that we had no future.

But we don't cry and for different reasons. He can't
      be seen with the weakness
      of a woman. And I don't cry
      because it's dangerous to be
      woman. In this foreign land
      we call home, a teardrop
      gets tattooed at the corner
      of our eye to let the world
      know that you don't
      have to go far to fight a war.

San Quentin Senryu

Building a prison

in a beautiful place

act of kindness or cruelty

Christopher Cunningham

GO

it makes no difference
how you paint,
just paint.
it makes no damn difference
how the clay
is lumped and shaped and smoothed,
just
sculpt.
it makes no difference
if it drips or runs
or rolls over
or screams or
begs or tears or
breaks in half or in a million
pieces or
dies or weeps or yearns
or hurts
or leaves or stays or
returns.

play your instrument:
too many of us

on this turning rock
only hold the thing
in our timid hands,
waiting for it to play
itself.

Christopher Cunningham

carve the words
even if your fingers
bleed from the flowers
in the stone.

last meal of the night

he looks at me with
red eyes
through thick round
glasses, heavy black frames
slipping forward
on his human nose.

it is two minutes until closing.

I tell him,
"go ahead man, what do you need?"

the kitchen grumbles, I can feel
anger rising upon my neck in
hot tired waves.

he mercifully orders
the easiest thing on the menu.

his will be our last meal of the night.

the cook is fast, throws it to me
and I bag it up.
he reaches out to take it
and asks me my name.

I tell him.

he then reaches to shake my hand.

Christopher Cunningham

"I know you are trying to close
but I really needed this food.
my brother is up the street
at the university hospital
and he is
probably going
to die tonight.

he is still holding my hand and I can see
his eyes, the space beyond his eyes, shielded
sort of by the thick lenses,
grow wider

but not very much.

"thank you for your kindness."

he drops my hand and is gone.

the hunger
we cannot stand to bear
alone,
but must.

the lateness of the hour

picking out
avocados
and limes
under the
teeming and
throbbing angel light
of
miles long
fluorescent tubes.

the floor
reflects
silently
upon this

as
two teenage girls
try to
buy
a bottle of
wine
and are turned away.

good to find
out early
that
nothing
is
going

Christopher Cunningham

to go
exactly
as you'd like.

that is,
unless you
are after
nothing.

the avocados weren't
very fresh,
but the limes
were
beautiful in the light.

horrors of the wet morn

a wet, black
sock riding
in a
black leather
shoe standing in
a deep puddle
at
9:27 a.m.
with rain coming down
and

a lifetime
to go.

Christopher Cunningham

dawn

I like sitting
in a dark room
with the lights off
as the sun
is just coming up.
with the blankets over the panes,
the light only has a thin slit
at the top
thru which
to enter
and
that faint bluegreen glow
starts before
you could ever see it,
even with the best of eyes.

I like that

and the silence
of the

dew.

it only lasts for a second
but
often

a second
can
mean the difference
between
small victories
and smaller defeats.

bending, but not the other

a weeping cherry
tree
that I pass on
my way to work
has contracted
a tree disease;

at the top,
it is dying.

the signs are obvious,
and the small
area that is infected
will
spread.

it is spring time,
and
the sun is high
and
the drive to work is
easy and good,

never mind the job.

I pass that
weeping cherry
and
can see,

below the sickness,

underneath the inevitable,

despite what comes,

flowers.

blue mouse

so
like
the footprint
of a ghost,
a tiny hiccup
of blue smoke
curling
around itself

in the pine straw
and acorns.

pearls of dew
reflect the grey dawn.

the air is very still.

over damp earth
a
hawk's shadow
crawls.

the precision
of time.

this space
between
here and there.

Christopher Cunningham

small deaths
and
larger tragedies.

a circle
tightening.

a sure thing

I
pour another
glass
of Bordeaux
at four fifty-five a.m.
and listen
to the wind.

leather and rubies
and smoke
on my tongue
with the breath
of winter
condensing
on the glass
of my small window.

they say there may be
bad weather
on the horizon.

I am sure there is.

the wind speaks
of strangers dressed in black
of loaded pistols
of broken guitars
of failed attempts
and worn boot heels.

Christopher Cunningham

I am listening
to the
harmony
of violence and wine.

I keep one red eye
on
the
window

and one on the glass.

the animals

every cubicle
is
a slaughterhouse.

each alarm clock
is
a whirring knife.

the television
is a
trough.

it is
always feeding time.

and
each
and
every
day

there is killing to be done.

Christopher Cunningham

a song in the night like a laugh

at
four a.m.
I can hear
a
mockingbird
singing
outside
my covered window.

he sits in
the darkness
singing
the songs
of other birds

but he weaves them together
in a song
of his own.

he is laughing
with stolen music.

he is the
only
music
out
there.

I listen.

college park, georgia

compressed waves of
bass
crawl rapidly
along the ground.

they are absorbed
by panes of window glass
vibrating in their frame.

it soon recedes,
a waning moon of sound
in a desolate sky.

gunshots
are
merely punctuation
to
unspoken sentences.

unguarded

I watch a junkyard dog
tossing a long piece of
bright red rubber
into the air
and pouncing upon it,
snapping it back and forth
in his teeth
then jumping around
like a hyperactive child
and doing it again.

the dog is supposed to
be patrolling the
grounds of a
cheap used car lot
in a rundown section of
town.

but instead
the dog is playing.

occasionally
even the savage beasts
among us
can laugh.

it gives me
some small measure of
hope
as I
move forward

into it.

down this crooked road

we strike out
for
the horizon.

we know not
what
the weather will
bring.

we
are almost ill-prepared
but
there
is madness
and daring
in our eyes
as
we cut ties
and

stare back
at
the
abyss,

laughing.

Miles J. Bell

Half-full for me despite my protestations to the contrary

So if as it seems
the wages of hope
are disappointment
and cynicism's
just not worth it
how then to pull off
the balancing act
on a thin wire
6 feet from
nothing at all?

modern life
some sage said
is rubbish
the world compels us
to find fault with ourselves
the things we fill the gaps with
are never enough
and reaching is dangerous
fingernails removed by satellites
beaming advertisements
into our illusive emptiness

not to be carried away
by excesses of happiness
or misery
we're told
is the only safe path

but all I want in this
blink-of-an-eye life
is to not reach the end
fighting for
one
last
breath
thinking only
life was everything
I expected

and
less.

Unlucky

The soft, disappointed yellow
of old streetlamps
twinkles from every imperfection
on this frozen road.
Stars on the ground.
All those pennies
I never picked up.

Miles J. Bell

She watches him eat

like it's going out of fashion.
But passionless, filling a hole
where a man should be. She wonders
what little changes she could have made
to make things better then or now
or at least different somehow.

He wonders why she's always staring,
wishing she would just sit down.
When she stands he can see all of her.
The photographs of when she was younger
will always be prettier.
She only smiles for visitors -

if only he could go out and come
back in again. She should love him,
even with grease around his mouth
and crumbs on his chin. Now she's
suspicious when he wears aftershave.
He only uses it on office days.

Love the night

2 kids pass
striding into town
I know that feeling
nowhere to be just
a twenty in yr pocket
& some real cigarettes
ready to murder the darkness
with laughter & stories
nothing but almost-free time
stretching before you with
eyes full of promise but
a steel heart where
nothing gets in or out
you can love the night but
it never loves you back
& you have to accept
it's always in
the company of darkness
time flashes by
& the end of a good thing
comes too soon
the eyes are now
endless & empty
black & cold
but the day
begins
like a prayer
to keep that darkness away
light surges into you

Miles J. Bell

like a shot of something good
& it's something pure & true
and you know
like love & pain & all of us
it will eventually
fade to shadow
but yr happy anyway
for now
I think yes
I used to know that feeling

The good and the wise lead quiet lives

The whole world's a
noisy place these days.

A phone bleeps
in an infested shopping arcade
and everyone checks
irrespective of whether
they heard their own individual
tone.

Music plays for three quarters of a minute
from the PA system
before another advert for a product
you don't want to buy
but can't do without.

Every shop has its own version
of music or
something almost like it.

Conversation is impossible
and becomes loud
ugly and
cyclical.

At these moments
all I want
is an old man's pub
before they banned smoking

and watch the sunlight hold my breath
in its warm hands.

Maybe a jukebox
turned low.

The clink of glasses
as afternoon ambles towards evening.

And the hardest thing to decide
is whether this pint
should be followed by another
or a quiet walk
towards home

or something
almost like it.

Icarus Rex

I nearly
gave up I
never forgot
how to fly
just didn't think
it worth
doing...

this maze of streets
suffocates in summer sweat
slides down spines
air choked with scents
of gently burning value burgers
and brittle forced bonhomie
later thoughts will turn
to the watering holes of the "Gaza" Strip
the waterfront apocalypse
of chain pubs and pointless kickings
angry minotaurs stalk the bars
slurping down their stupid suds
somebody else's accident
waiting to happen
                    this
is the 21st century
incendiary lifestyles
for emotional cripples
and social chameleons

there will be casualties

and Gibbo moves with all the grace
of a knife fight in a phonebox
stares
at shiny faces
families
in new saloons meandering
along the beaten seafront
knowing it's too big a gap
to cross between them and him
they see
one of those funny chavs
you read about them all the time
tonight Matthew I will be
compartmentalizing
dehumanizing
who's afraid of the big bad dole boy
if you laugh at what you're afraid of
it might go away
(shamefully
I do it, too)
Gibbo feels but could never articulate
an imaginary conversation
between these people and himself
I'll stay out of your dreams
if you stay out of mine
but even these car radios blare
In every dream home a heartache
into this anodyne world

where any kind of fame

is more sought after and celebrated
than any sort of kindness
or happiness
commodity over community
possession is 9/10
of the new lore
in the Iron Pyrite dreams
of this proud new millennium
glittering prizes to
own own own
which bleeds into
self self self
here's a new chest freezer
you don't really need it
but join us and you've made it
love the higher power
all on hire purchase
subliminal product placement
and blatant hard sell
hello hello
this is a good buy
time to get that 2nd motor
for your neighbors as much as anyone
free to do every bit
of what you're told
like a good consumer
we are the champions
no time for losers
this is how the world ends
not with a bang
but a whisper

of a sale
capitalism:
the gentle holocaust
a subtle strangling

there will be casualties

I only drink so much
so I can stop the ticking
for a little while
of what the French call
La Tristesse de la Vie -
the sadness of life -
and also because these days
I write best
with a hangover.
This will eventually kill me.
But anything can kill you:

A mother and her 12 year old
autistic son were feared dead
yesterday after they disappeared.
She left a note saying she thought
she'd failed as a mother and
her and Ryan were going to the bridge
so the family wouldn't have to worry
anymore. She hadn't taken
her medication with her.
CCTV footage taken at
3 pm yesterday appears to show
two figures falling from the 150m bridge

eight seconds apart
and what must she have felt
standing in the light
for the last time
before that forever drop
into darkness
she had balls
and a lot of heart
but in the end
it wasn't quite enough
and did she pray
for no life flashing
behind her closed eyes
in the rushing silence
all those years
drowning in the sun

I listen to other people's conversations:

- she's so fat
- yeah but I bet
she sweats when she fucks
- I bet she sweats
when she eats
- I can't believe
it's not Buddha

sometimes the apocalypse
can't come quick enough
sometimes
just an ordinary gull

wheeling overhead
can lift a day
the miracle of flight
of wings and hearts
let the missiles fly
and turn them into
circling birds
then I might
believe

but tonight
this sopping club
is holding
far more gurning
hatchet-faced simpletons
than seems possible
a real retardis
everybody
fired up
pilled up
the music can't be
loud enough
every desperate
flailing dancer
chasing that mad rush
when the bass kicks in
and takes your head
clean off we're
chasing ultimate highs
and maybe
this is love

chasing anything
except
tomorrow morning
then the lights are on
music dies
disappointed silence
and out
into the heart of town
the heart of darkness
tell me who prays
for the soul of a taxi queue?
one couple waits
slumped against
wet brickwork
her eyes are
almost open
staring past the world
in an alcopop reverie
his head in hands
laces undone
and puke on his shirtfront
a private apocalypse
in this public hell
someone in line
sticks the nut on someone's mate
and it all kicks off
stay still
don't catch anyone's eye:
the opposite
of all you've done
this evening

you don't even
breathe out
until the cab is
speeding you
from all that darkness
and into
the welcoming night

nothing in the battered
paracetemol packet but
instructions for use
and throbbing nothing
but holes in my pockets
sometimes hope can fall
right out of your life
as easily as
anything else
this painful pulse
the only way I know
I'm awake
and arguably
alive
I watch the second hand
go round and round and round
and wait for nothing to happen
and nothing does

I listen to other people's conversations:

- *Get to the fuckin bar cunt*
am spi-ing fevvuhs

the time I felt most alive:
in the open space
of the grey heath in New Cross
with fast friends
watching
the mother of all thunderstorms roll in
forks tearing down the sky
chewing through burning ozone
drunk and exhilarated
standing on the bench
arms wide
as the storm came
holding bottle and cigarette
screaming
come on come on come on
urging the world louder
the rain faster
waiting for
a perfect death
and ready to defy
god himself

I've felt shivers of wonder at the alien spires
of the Church of the Sagrada Familia
I've seen a grown man punch a five year old
square in the face for dropping an ice cream
I've drunk tequila sunrises at 5 pm on a pub bench
winking at the businesswomen
I've spoken with the ghost of Primo Levi
and asked him how he made it and he said

I didn't
I've chased a sunset for hours on a plane to New
York while trying to forget I was on a plane
I've seen the news every day every day every day
I have loved the stars too well to fear the night

At the wake
my grandma thanked me for coming
and said how smart I looked
in my suit. Smiled
as she said she hoped
I'd come to see her again
like we were arranging something
out of the ordinary.
But on the way out
her face became desperate
as she held on to me
and she said
- I keep sitting in his chair
so I don't have to look at it
and for once in my life
I didn't have anything to say.

I listen to other people's conversations:

- She had a cunt like a kebab
that's been kicked all the way home

I must stop listening to other people's conversations

what to make, then

of this ever-subtle
maddening sensual
fragile frame
which houses the muscle
that can move the world?
That conjures
symphonies and sicknesses
births dancehalls and Dresdens?
The only thing I can do
is make garlands of words
and hang them around the shoulders
of everyone I meet
forever
because in the end
I'd rather go down
burning and laughing
than trundle tamely
into that goodnight
a static prisoner
of the days and years
I'll take
a run at the sun
ripping at the darkness
with a pen and a wine
it's the only way to
fly.

2 kinds of nostalgia

6.30;
the sun has yet to
wrestle the night to one side
and the old ladies still dribble
into their floral quilts.

It's been so long
since I had a real hangover
I can almost welcome it
like a friend of a friend you used to see a lot of
don't like much
but find fascinating.

Last night I rediscovered
the simple joys of loud music in headphones
while pacing, glass of wine nearby
and a stupid fat smile on my face.
There may have been some air-guitar moments.

I was choosing music for my wedding party
while Em did the same on the PC
in the other room.

I didn't even have any dinner
and those of you that know my silhouette will confirm
I miss meals as often as I miss
the cyst on my right ball I had drained
in 1989.

What with t.v. and the Wii and
lots of early nights I haven't played my favourite songs
in a long time
but such a gorgeous cacophony!

Dinosaur Jr and Dizzee Rascal and The Cardiacs
and Royksopp and The Maytals and
so on
with the volume so high
that when I turned off the stereo
my ears roared as if carrying on without it.

Later today the tiredness will drag me down
and when the baby cries and
cries next door
I will want it to grow up and leave home
and when the dog barks the same
note over and over from 2 doors down
I will want it to die.

I will be oil-skinned and rancid of tongue
and there will not be enough water
in the world.

Nevertheless I am determined
to enjoy the day as well as I can
and to remember (as if I needed reminding)
that the pain proves
you're alive.

I drank and danced like the world was ending last night
I slept like the dead
but this morning
the world is still here
and so
am
I.

William Taylor Jr.

Slow

It's true,
I am slow.

In most things.

I am slow as I type this,
hunting and pecking at the keys,
pausing between lines, words and letters

to look at my cat
or out the window at the cars passing by.

I will pause to look at an old photograph
or to listen to a song on the stereo.

I will pause to read part of a book
I have read many times before.

I will pause to do nothing at all
for minutes or hours.

Some days I try and wake early
telling myself I will get things done

and then the next thing I know
the sun will be late into the sky

and I will have little to show for the hours
that have passed.

William Taylor Jr.

I take a slow walk around the city
and feel more akin
to the trees and the buildings

than to the people.

The trees wave at me and I back at them,
understanding

there is so much in this life
not to do

and so little time not to do it in.

Christmas at The Brown Jug

You know the holidays are near
because Nadine wears gold sequins

and a mechanical snowman
dances on the bar

to the music on the juke.

The woman on the stool next to mine
drinks white Carlo & Rossi
in a pint glass over ice

and says, *we're all nice people here.*

The woman on the other side
has three teeth
wears a reindeer sweater

and declares
I am not an abomination, my sweet lord
loves me!

Outside
there's some kind of altercation,
strong words and threats of violence

despite the sign on the lamp post
declaring this a hate free zone

and you can already hear the sirens.

An old yellow sign always hangs above the bar
saying

FREE BEER TOMORROW.

It's funny
if you think about it.

Rainy Afternoon

The rain comes down
on a Sunday afternoon
in San Francisco.

It's as good a day as any to sit in a bar
and watch the world go by,

as good a day as any

to take back just a little bit
of what the world forever steals.

Me, I get drunk at the Gold Cane
as the tourists and the hipsters
drift up and down
the avenue.

A true smile from a stranger is enough
to set things right
for a little while.

I drink it in

and let the bitterness slide off
like rain down a windowpane

that looks out on Haight Street
on a rainy afternoon
in San Francisco.

John Berryman, They Say

Before jumping off the
Washington Avenue Bridge

John Berryman, they say,
waved goodbye
to a passing stranger.

Now
say what you will
about the man,
his art
and the right to
or wrongness of
suicide:

style,
you must admit,
is important in such matters.

I Bet They Never

Wise men say it's good to know
when to let go of things

but I bet they never saw you
in that dress

stretched out on the damp grass

with the late afternoon sun
shining

down
just so.

William Taylor Jr.

The Heat

It was a strangely hot
day in San Francisco
and I stretched out in the cool
grass of the park with a
cheap six pack

along with all the others
with nothing
better to do.

The feel of the sun
the grass
and the cold
cold beer

was as good as anything
the world had to offer.

A shirtless man
not much older than myself
sat down beside me.

He said nothing
and I said nothing
and we sat that way
for a while.

I've been sober for ten days,
he finally said,
and I don't much see the point.

I smiled a bit
in reply.

Mind if I have one of those,
he asked, motioning
toward the beer.

I nodded and handed him
a bottle.

He popped the cap and took a long drink.

It's good, he said.

Indeed, I replied.

The heat, he continued,
makes it hard
to do anything.

But then I guess
that's life,

all you can do
is relax a bit
and wait for it
to pass.

The heat, I asked,
or life?

Whichever,
he replied.

Madness

It is much easier than
we imagine;
a door left ajar
a thread about to snap
a string to be pulled
a black core at the heart
of the sun
a simple giving in
a little letting go
a tapping at our window panes
at 4 a.m.
we are closer to it
than we recognize
we understand it
more then we will say
we long for it
in dreams we will never
speak of.
It speaks to me now
in a language that smells
of winter rain
and of all things lost and
dreaming to be
found.

A Truth I Could Only Imagine

A young black girl
sits in a doorway
near the fire house.

She is talking to herself
or god
or somebody I can't see.

Her eyes are wide
as she gesticulates wildly
with skinny arms

saying

This feels like hell
this looks like hell
this smells like hell

I tell you man
we are all
in hell.

And here I was thinking
it was a decent enough
Wednesday afternoon

in downtown
San Francisco.

But those eyes of hers
had an authority
I could not deny;

they knew a truth
I could only imagine.

I met them a moment
and then looked away

the sun's fire
bearing down

and all the sirens wailing.

A Fool With a Four Dollar Frappachino

This used to be a German beer garden
and now it's a Starbucks coffeehouse,
and I sit here like a fool
with a four dollar frappachino instead of a beer.

A tired sun shines down
and I am thinking of all that has been
swept away
by powers I will never understand,
only to be replaced with
cheaper things, all
sad and new and hollow.

It seems an endless and
ongoing process,
tiring and without
reason.

I watch a tattooed girl
lean upon a lamppost
smoking in the afternoon sun.

I think:
this at least is something,
all is not yet lost.

Moments later
the girl drops her cigarette
on the pavement,

William Taylor Jr.

adjusts her skirt
and moves on,

something less beautiful
filling her space.

The Strangest

It's the strangest thing
to wake each morning and find
you still exist;

to wake from one dream to a stranger one

to find your hands are still there
your feet and your belly
and the rest of you

your face in the mirror
just as you remembered it

to once again be
trapped inside a self
you have no idea
what to do with.

And the longer the dream lasts
the stranger it becomes.

It's strange to see the people around you
going about their business
with a seeming confidence

as if there were nothing frightening
strange or funny
about walking and talking
about putting on shoes

William Taylor Jr.

and driving cars on freeways
about buying loaves of bread
and having wives and husbands and children

as if there were nothing absurd
in any of it

as if living
and dying
were perfectly sensible states of being

and waking each day
to find you still exist
wasn't the strangest
goddamned thing.

The Insect

The window was open
and something that looked like a
small green grasshopper
crawled in and
walked around and
waved its feelers at me.

I watched it awhile
and noticed what a pleasant shade
of green it was,
like new spring grass
or something flavored lime.
I noticed it was missing a leg
but it didn't seem too concerned.

When I was done watching I decided
to put it back outside
so it wouldn't die.

Moments later I looked up
to see it caught in the web
of a large and ugly spider
just outside my window.

Perhaps I should have seen this
as symbolic of some greater truth
concerning life and death
and the general way of things,
but I only felt responsible somehow,

so I pulled it free and wished it well.

I sat back down to write this poem
which I offer up for luck
for the insect, myself,
and all the rest of you.

Mickey's Place

Mickey lived next door
to the house I grew up in,
the house where my mom still lives.

He had lived there all my life,
all his life.
He must be close to fifty now.

Some years ago he moved out
of the main house and into
a little trailer that sat in the driveway.

Mickey lived in that trailer for twenty some years.

Every time I would go back home
to visit mom,
Mickey would be standing in the door
of his little trailer in the driveway,
smoking a cigarette and drinking
a can of beer.

"Hey, Billy," he would greet me.

"Hey, Mickey," I'd reply.

The last time I went home
Mickey's trailer was there
but Mickey was not.

William Taylor Jr.

The door to his trailer was closed
and on it was posted a sign
that said in the name of some city ordinance or
other
this residence has been condemned.

A few other signs were posted about the trailer
that said similar things.

I walked into my house and said to my mom,

"Where's Mickey?"

"The people came and told him
he couldn't live there, anymore,"
she said,
"about two weeks ago. They said it was
uninhabitable."

"Where did he go," I asked.

"For a few nights he slept
on a cot on the porch
and then he was gone."

I couldn't think of anything to say.

"And did you hear about Emma,"
Mom asked.

Emma was Mickey's mom.

"No," I said, "what?"
"She's got the Alzheimer's. You'd hardly
know her anymore."

"That's a shame," I said.

I had never much cared for Emma,
or her family in general, but still.

We talked a while more and then mom
went to bed.

I opened the fridge and found a beer.

I sat out in the backyard
in one of my dead father's old chairs

and listened to the crickets

as everything dead, living, or in-between
on this unquiet earth
moved slowly toward its end.

Bad Night

It was just one of those nights.
I just wandered the streets
feeling generally bad
in search of a quiet place
to drink beer and listen to sad music
on the jukebox.

I found a place that looked
okay
got a stool
and a beer
and things were alright
for a little while

until a fellow sat down next to me
and started to talk.
He was middle aged and red faced
and looked as if he spent
most of his waking hours in bars.
I ignored him as best I could
until it was finally impossible.

You work at that one place, right,
the music store?

Yes, I replied in a manner
meant to suggest I had no desire
to discuss the matter any further.

I bet you listen to a lot of music, he said.

I guess so.

What kind of music you listen to?

I dunno. Lot's of stuff.

You like punk rock, the Clash and shit?

Sure.

You like the Floyd? Led Zeppelin?

Floyd, yeah. Fuck Zeppelin.

You wear a lot of Black. You like Johnny Cash?

Sure.

What about Elvis?

Costello?

Naw, man, Presley. Elvis. The King.

I don't care about Elvis, I said.

You look like somebody who likes Elvis.

Fuck Elvis.

You like to swing dance?

No, man. Look, no offense, but can we please stop
    talking now?

You can't have a haircut like that and not like to

swing dance.

I just want to drink my beer. Please go away.

Ah, shit, it's cool, man. I'm just making conversa-
tion, that's all.

Please stop talking now.

The man gave me a funny look
as if he had never met anyone in a bar
who didn't want to talk to him
then got up walked a few stools down
and started in with somebody else.

Things were okay again
I was able to finish my beer
and order another
before someone else sat down beside me.

He started talking as well.

I excused myself for a moment,
Promising to return.

I walked to the back of the bar
used the bathroom
then slipped out the back door.

I picked a direction and walked.

You know it's a bad night
when you can't even find a bar
to be lonely in.

It is Enough

I can't tell you just what it is
I'm looking for today;

not hope, exactly,
but a little sign from the world
that life
is sometimes more
than simply
waiting on death.

I watch for such moments.

Like right now;
there is something
in the girl sitting at the table in the
afternoon sun,

with her sunglasses and her pint of beer,
cigarette held just so,
a cheap paperback novel open in front of her.

I cannot say what it is,
I cannot put a name to it
but it is there;

a hint of possibility
in the curve of her mouth
and in the patterns the sunlight makes
upon the tabletop.

It is enough,
it is all I ask.

I breathe it in
and believe.

Christopher Robin

Saved

my lover arrives with a litany:
the kid with fetal alcohol syndrome
and his abusive parents,
her mother with dementia,
the French immigrant,
(her husband),
lonely, jealous-
all I want is to be quiet
and just make out-
we lay together in my bed
in the dark , kissing,
not letting go
but not doing much more
her phone rings
friend in a wheelchair is
drinking again,
crying-
she answers:
"Alcoholism is the easiest thing in the world to cure!
Once you quit, it's easy! You'll be healthy again!
You can do anything!"
I want to tell her most of that is a damn lie
but I keep my mouth shut-
after the 3rd call
she hangs up,
and crawls between my legs-
she's saved me more than once
and sometimes lying quietly
or quietly lying
is the best a man can do

Christopher Robin

On the Assumption of My Usefulness
(for Silvi-Ann)

I am not one hundred percent able-bodied
nor all that mentally astute
I don't assemble anything more complex
than instant oatmeal-
to the degree that I am useful
for people less competent than I
(mainly the elderly and the very rich)
I get paid for it-
and further
I don't move furniture for friends, only clients
and again, I get paid-
and also
I only assemble fish tanks for women
I am sleeping with
and since I know nothing
about assembling
fish tanks
or broken women
I am currently celibate
and will most likely remain so-
that is until fish
or women can evolve
or de-evolve enough
so that
a half cup of oats, a half cup of water
and half a man
are all that's required
for their survival

Girls Don't Look

and boys laugh at me from across the train tracks

"fuck you bitch"

I am far away by then

hauling my electric scooter up the stairs to my rat trap

low income loser 12 miles an hour unless its windy

but girls man

they pat my head

they use words like "adorable" and call me "kiddo"

and the phone solicitors feel sorry for me
they call me 'ma'am'
"I'm sorry you're so angry MA'AM
that we charged 49.95 on your credit card,
MA'AM, but wait…."

I can't go to the animal shelter because I cry

because I will never have a dog

I gave up my best girl

she was going to get me a dog and a house in the country

Christopher Robin

she wanted me to be responsible

she thinks responsibility is having a beard, working
    at a construction site and raising a future serial
    killer that eats his own boogers

I think responsibility is saying out loud: "I'M A KID
    FOREVER I LIKE THE PASSENGER SIDE OF
    THE CAR I TRAVEL WITH A STUFFED ANI-
    MAL I'M INCAPABLE OF UNCONDITIONAL
    LOVE I BUY TOO MANY LOTTERY TICK-
    ETS I SCRATCH WHERE I SHOULDN'T BE
    SCRATCHING MY HOUSE ISN'T BIG ENOUGH
    FOR A BRAT IT'S ONLY BIG ENOUGH FOR A
    BRAT LIKE ME"

and I want to end this poem by saying I need love
and companionship just like everyone else
gosh I'm only human
and admit
that I was once a selfish bastard
but now all the love songs make sense
but that's not true
not true at all and   I am not sorry   not one bit

How to Turn an SSI Check into Pimpin'

the rusty wheels of the free Caddy rumble
through the neighborhoods of give and take
homeless friend works with me in the yards
from the yards I get clothing, snacks and
strange gifts
which I pass on to the Soft Poet
who feeds me bowls of noodles and tuna fish
that look oddly familiar

this is bottom of the food chain livin'
meals shared, arguments embraced,
books passed on, poetry, poetry, poetry
a well cultivated economy of style and
unspoken divinity

we labor here as sinners, liars,
gentle hustlers and rogues
barefoot and carefree
on undernourished American soil
the economic free fall
freeways collapsing
feverish waters rising
infrastructure buckling

friends inside these yellow walls
will wail against the Mayan calendar
and our few short years
imploring me to leave with them
to France, Canada, Italy

Christopher Robin

but love and goodness hold the last house key-
all I have to do is scratch and wait

I remain unscarred
by the anti-social engineering
of the welfare system
lovers come to cook and I
eat everything
men and women, with honey on my
lips
I smoke and serenade them with sarcasm
and false hope
shaking down apple trees
and lonely housewives on the west side

social worker says I need motivation
to wake, to bathe, to learn
but I have been lying to social workers
and lying down with angels

Freaky Mumbler's Manifesto

I'd like to tell you I stayed
up all night
shadow boxing with the Muse
creating
rock and roll poems
that will topple empires
or that Oprah called to say
I wasn't really just a fat
hairy loser
and asking how
did I ever transform
the misfortune
of my birth
and my own profound
stupidity
to become the artist
I am today
and that she
wanted to give me a car
on national TV
to show the world
that half-wit trannies
are a gift
not a detriment
to society
but instead I will tell you this:
staying up all night
touching one's self
does not a genius make

and trannie just aint that sexy
no matter what the enlightened say
and sometimes being DUMB
is just being DUMB
and being broke is no reason to gloat
and being smelly is not revolutionary
and being confused is just
BEING CONFUSED
not having a day job
never made me an artist
it's just one more day
of bad coffee
bad skin
unshaven
no sex
one more day of trying not to wish
I was smart or good looking
or employed
because you know it's not very poetic
to wish for such things
but far more entertaining
to bleed the blues
all over the dirty carpet
create a new alphabet
of some sort of deranged redemption
and strike a one-two punch
for all the wage slaves
who can't afford to be literary
so I'm sorry Oprah
I don't have any visions
there is just nothing supernatural

about being out of Half and Half
and not having showered by 3 o'clock
and I'm out of toilet paper and
I don't know what to do
should I write a poem?
should I eat?
should I kill myself?
or should I just figure out
how to wipe my own ass first?
there's just no key
for this sort of thing
no cosmic blueprint
nothing extraordinary
about this day
this life
this poem
Freak Town is not a tourist destination
it's the end of the line
nobody's giving out any prizes
it's not hip
and no one's cleaned the bathroom
in 6 years

Christopher Robin

Infinite Joy In Spite Of

when the electricity comes back
when he gets a job
when the barbed wire is gone
when the food stamps come
when all the kittens are placed
when the three kids are raised
when their mother gets clean
when the shooting stops
and the fires are out
when the sun breaks through
and the beach isn't contaminated
when the prisoners stop writing
and the interviews done
when gasoline drops
and the exits reopen
when the war is over
and democracy wakes up
after my neighbors are fed
the calls returned
the bills paid
the coffee cold
and cigarettes extinguished
I still won't be done-
        exhausted
        bitter
        joyous I sleep.

Slingshot

The poetry of the streets has a slingshot
aimed right at your cozy metaphor
the poetry of damaged youth
whizzes by on a skateboard
with a perpetual hard on for Lady Luck
but she won't flash her tits
for just anyone
the poetry of no risk
refuses to get a tattoo
just in case it
decides one day to
get a real job
and can finally move out of mothers basement
the poetry of contemplating garden snails
has too long admired its own belly button
the poetry of self-infatuation
will honor itself with a 15 minute parade
while the patrons of the Open
Mic try to chew their own legs off
the ghost of Joey Ramone
runs with scissors
through the gardens of nostalgia
snipping the dead-heads
from warbling hippie roses
the poetry of the streets says:
here is a bag lady
with a head full of wind chimes
throw your sonnets out the window
and feed her-

Christopher Robin

the poetry of the streets
turned Lenny Bruce into Christ
timeless poetry knows deep down
the time is now
but flesh and time are both liars
and that God
does not really love the meek-
and only the slam poets
will inherit the earth

I Want to Be a Better Asshole

94 year old Italian lady wants to know have I been sick?
yes, I lie
 I don't want to work
so I am just waiting for her to die
it's so much easier than telling the truth
another writer wants to read me three pages of her short
        story
please no! I say
and then there is the one who will talk about his novel
        for an hour
never once asking if I am getting any writing done
it almost makes me welcome the other half dozen calls
asking me to order the "Girls Gone Wild" DVD-
ask me if I care
whether the featured Friday night poet
gets beaten by her old man
a Nazi-looking-motherfucker/half deaf who stands
in the corner scowling the whole evening
and she too timid to read
or do I wonder if the one in the small hotel is eating-
getting paid for her short stories with anything
other than contributors copies
which don't fry up as nicely as the eggs I crack
on a Sunday afternoon
singing and crying to the voice
of the 19 year old boy
who had a nervous breakdown
and doesn't sing at our venue anymore
or the poet with the flu that

Christopher Robin

I just kicked back to the woods
"my cabin is cold" he says "and I have to get
well enough to go back to work or I'll get fired"
or she who asks:
do you like me better manic or depressed
or do you like me at all?
and I don't know what to say-
at the end of the world should we demand or es-
    chew civility?
and if we're all so broken
how can we put each other back together?
and how many volumes of poetry
will it take to end these wars, dig us
out of the economic scrap heap
and close the gaping wounds?

Searching for Joan of Ark in Front of Safeway

didn't I take you to buy white candles
and salt when the evil spirits
were getting into your
underwear drawer
and moving your paintings around?
when the apartment became possessed
you left your beloved cat, Romeo, behind
and disappeared-
I didn't see you for two years
my oldest friend, the witch
who always told the story
of meeting me for the first time
under the San Carlos street bridge
nearly twenty years ago
roasting potatoes under an overturned shopping cart-
you were working as a chef at a high class hotel-
now I see you head low, hair matted
a sunburned face outside of Safeway
I hug you
I kiss your head
you offer me a handful of white pills
no thanks, I say
do you want to go back on lithium?
well, they are shooting lasers into my teeth see?
there's a chip
its Revelations you know
I know
it's all in the bible
I know

Christopher Robin

I will take you to the hospital right now
and then I will feed you and give you a shower...
feel that
my belly she says
it's metal
where they tore out my insides
and see my teeth
those are microchips
see that TV across the street
if you go over there
I'm on it

Too Much Me

I go to the art galleries
I go to the anarchist café
I ingratiate myself *everywhere*
I want a large group of every-bodies
bleating poetry
about this burdened end of the block
I am annoying
smelly old bird with floppy shoes
I am your best advocate
you nobodies
you delicious slack happy dirty kids
I think I am the Love Nut
from a Ferlinghetti poem
I think I am history
I try and tip well-
my friends who aren't quite anarchists
my friends who aren't quite punks
my friends who are middle class
and everywhere in between
working class and worthless.....
I am too aggressive at lemonade stands
I want to hold up tiny businesses with my SSI checks-
I expect that you are open-handed too
perhaps I believe in you too much
because you seem hapless and foolhardy
sometimes I believe these fly by night dashes of faith
will last forever
like a child's summer evening-
they will fill the holes on the avenue
with vicious hotels and condos
serving none of us
if we don't fill them first

Christopher Robin

Who We Kill

The mentally ill
Who wave water pistols
The blacks who wave wallets
And can't surrender fast enough
The animals that weren't cute enough
The animals that made the mistake
Of being born delicious...
The trannies that can't hide
The mistake of being born wrong...
The self-taught publishers
Who overflow the toilets
In the Borders bathroom
The lone poet
Who furiously walks the streets
Thinking maybe around the next corner
The world will show me some light
The service workers who spend their pay
In the local bars
And their imaginations on satellite dishes
The prisoners who make our goods for no pay...
The muddy trumpet players
With their songs of drowning
On America's rooftops....
The musty bookstores of my childhood
With shelves that went on forever
And kept me from the taunting of schoolmates...
The roadside fruit stands
We passed on our way to Christmas in Soledad-
The high rents here will send my friends away:

The potters who can't sell their pots
Musicians whose notes are out of time
Poets who can't sell their revolutionary poem
For a crust of bread from a birds beak
We're not the chosen ones
And nobody's buying anyway
So get on SSI or find a better hustle,
A barn, a roach-infested shoebox
At the El Palomar
Or maybe a room at El Centro
Where they didn't find the body
And the fluids dripped through the floor
Into the restaurant below...
And there's always that old standby
The bridge behind Denny's
Where I used to drink coffee
Crawl into my bag
And scribble poetry onto the concrete wall
Not waiting for a publisher
Just the light of day

Father Luke

Come Home

Outside my window,
and four stories down,
there's a tree without leaves.
A sweatshirt is hanging
from one of its branches.
Looking up from the street,
you could see me
a guy pulling out a draw from a smoke.
Every now and again
a light like an orange firefly.

But you wouldn't see the years.
"Come home!"
"No."
"Please?"
"Give me one good reason why."
"Your clothes are killing the lawn."
It's an old song,
and many have heard it sung.
And tonight
I am home.
And I'm wondering whose clothes are
killing that lawn tonight.

Father Luke

It Will Never Be My Turn

once again I'm facing the end of the month without
a job and without rent money.

I'm listening to music in my hotel room.
i feel a coastal breeze,
and taste the salt in the air.

I'm nearly 50 years old,
and I'm beginning to
understand:

it will never be my turn.

Holes In the Shadows

tonight there was an earthquake
it was fairly decent sized
i live on the fourth floor of an old hotel.

after the earthquake i stood out in the hallway
watching everyone.

a few people
poked their heads into the hallway
i waved. they smiled, and closed the door.

one guy lives in a room down the hallway from his
mother.
that guy ran to his mother's room to see about her.

i watched a woman i had fucked years ago,
run into her room. sex has always been something
which separates us.

"Did you feel it?" she said as she ran by me.
"that was a long time ago," i said to her. "let it go."
she gave me a little huff,
and she slammed her door.

i love moments like that.
i just love them.

Father Luke

With a Seagull For Company

Little Bob the crab died tonight.
I looked for him to be sitting on his log in the aquar-
    ium across the room. The aquarium light is the
    only light in the room when I come home. I
    didn't see Little Bob. I saw the plants waving in
    the current, and Little Bob should have been sit-
    ting on top of the log. That's his spot.
I took off my coat, dropped it on the floor, put my
    hat onto a lamp, and I walked across the room to
    look at the tank.
Big Bob the crab was sitting inside the log. That's
    Big Bob's favorite spot.
Hi Big Bob.
Big Bob tucked himself against the side of the log.
    Big Bob has post traumatic stress syndrome. Big
    Bob lost two legs on his left side, and he doesn't
    do well with the whole socializing thing.
On the on the other hand, Little Bob is the original
    party animal. I got him from a woman in the
    Hotel where I live - - she was going to throw him
    into the river.
He clipped a foot off my frog, she said.
She was holding a yogurt container. Inside, sitting
    on a wet tissue, I saw a crab not much bigger
    than my thumb. It waved a tiny claw in the air.
It kind of looked like he was goading me into fight-
    ing. I imagined I could hear Little Bob saying:
    C'mon. Let's fight, ya' dick head. I can take you,
    and five more just like you! Hippie! Faggot!
What if I took him, I said to the woman. I was still
    looking at the crab. I looked up at her. She

knew I had an aquarium. Take him, she said.

That's how I adopted Little Bob.

So, tonight I saw Little Bob lying on his back with his
legs in the air. They were moving in the current.
Okay. I get it, you're dead Little Bob. In death he
was still able to mock me.

I scooped him out with some chopsticks. Then I
wrapped him in a leaf from one of the plants in
my room. I tied it all together with another leaf.

Little Bob and I walked to the Santa Cruz Wharf in
the chill.

This is where you go on without me, Little Bob, I said.
I placed a coin in with Little Bob to pay his toll
across the river into Beulah Land. I owed him
that.

I reached my hand over the end of the pier, then into
the darkness, and let go. Little Bob was gone.

I sat down on one of the benches. A seagull walked
over to me. We heard the sea lions, and we lis-
tened to the waves.

Was it Little Bob, the seagull said to me.

Yeah, I said.

I'm sorry, said the seagull. He'll be missed.

Thanks, I said.

The seagull counted waves with me. Then he walked
away into the silence and the dark. I took a breath
of sea air and I smelled seaweed, and salt. I stood
up, adjusted the collar of my jacket, put my hands
in my pockets, and I walked back home.

Father Luke

Purpose

walking
to
work,
the sidewalks are wet

i look up at red and green leaves on the trees
along my way

i see the morning sky through the branches
it's soda pop orange
then i remember i'm on my way to work
and i hurry along

The Contender

There is a pain so full
that the rest of it doesn't matter.

It forms rings in your body
through the years, like the rings of a tree.

The wrinkles on your face,
which should be happy
reminders of laughs,
are instead a travel log
of sorrow, and of sadness, and of pain.

It's no use saying no to the years.
Fighting time is like wrestling with the air.

No isn't the answer.
And neither is yes.

There aren't any answers.
There are only the years, which
look at you from the other side of the room.

Fri3nd

"Hello. I am **m~ny:8s3v**,
and I want to be your friend."

The message is sitting there in my
inbox on the MySpace network.

I look up from the computer monitor
to the light shining on the walls,
and I feel a breeze coming in
from the dark night outside of my window.

My loneliness is a hollowness
in my bones which gives me sustenance
where the marrow should be,
and saying cocksucker for
no good reason makes me feel
really, really good . . .

Swearing has given
the ache of loneliness more
importance. I say. . . ". . . motherfucker,"
and the loneliness is happy — it's had its moment.

I approve **m~ny:8s3v**'s friend request,
and I walk to the kitchen for some soup.

Hi. It's Miguél

I had nine messages on my phone.

"Hi. It's me Gail…"

The way Gail says it fast it sounds like: "Hi. It's
    Miguél…"
"…I just wanted you to know I'll be leaving town for a
    while. I love you."

Gail is a crack whore I know. I know a lot of whores.
    I don't know why that surprises   some people.

Push the button.
Message erased.

"Father Luke, this is Lawrence's sister.
Can you give me a call collect? It's important."

There were some other messages. Gordy is ninety
    days sober and he's going bug-fuck nuts; my
    cousin Brad is in town wanting to get away from
    his mother – my Aunt, can he come over. Shit
    like that.

So, I call Lawrence's sister. I'm on Front Street, and
    I'm ordering Chile Rojo in a dirty Sombrero
    Mexican Restaurant. I'm fighting the flies for the
    cool air from the fan spinning slowly on squeaky
    ball bearings above my seat in the booth.

It's dark outside, and still very hot tonight.

"Hello, this is Father Luke."

"Father Luke, this is Lawrence's Sister."

I had called her, and so that didn't
come as too much of a surprise.

"Father Luke, Gail went to the bank the day my
        brother Lawrence died, and she withdrew nearly
        three thousand dollars."

Jeezus. "Has Gail called you?"

"Well, she wanted to come take care of me, I'm in a
        wheelchair. Father Luke, forgive me, but if I ever
        see her I'll have her hair hanging on my wall."

"Well, that's okay, dear. I don't mind hearing that."

"It just has me so upset."

"I'm sorry, dear."

"Okay, Father Luke. I'll let you eat dinner."

"Alright, dear. Buh bye."

"Good night Father Luke."

I looked at the Chile Rojo. It was cold. I let the flies
        have it, and I tipped the waiter two dollars. Then
        I walked out into the night.

Arizona Still Life

The sun was setting in Arizona, and the monsoon
    was trying
really hard to bust through the dusty air.

We were on our way.
Somewhere. I can't remember where.

Not much was ever spoken between us.
I think we liked it that way. I did anyway.

You were driving.
I was watching the sky.

I'm torn, you said.
I looked over at you, then I waited for more.

I'm torn between watching the lightening on the
    one side, and
the sunset on the other.

Then there wasn't anything else for a while.
It seemed to be enough, though.

Throw a Gun on the Casket

Grimes Patterson sat in a motel in some horse shit
town on the California coast. He waved a fly
from a piece of toast, and read the newspaper.

He'd been somebody. He'd robbed banks, kid-
napped for ransom. He was among the baddest
motherfuckers you'd ever seen.

The linoleum on the kitchen floor was ripped, and
coming up in more places than it decently
covered. What little was left was covered with
a smooth, brown and yellow, greasy dirtiness
that wouldn't let his socks slide as he walked.

Grimes Peterson took a bite of the toast, and he
folded the newspaper, and put it down on the
red formica table. As he chewed, he flicked a
cockroach off the wall. He watched it walk in
circles on the floor. Then he stepped on it. The
bug made a little snap as he put pressure on it.
He took another bite of toast.

The water in the tea kettle began boiling. Grimes
adjusted his bathrobe, and stood up to pour
some water into a white cup over a spoonful of
instant decaf.

The water mixed with the instant coffee, and made
brown foam. Grimes leaned against the cracked

enamel of the sink, and looked into the cup,
and drew a heart in the foam with a spoon. He
let his mind drift to nowhere, then he stirred
the heart into the coffee, and sat back down at
the table.

He sipped the coffee. Hot. Too hot. He blew across
the top of the cup, and watched the steam make
paisleys in rays of light filtered through vene-
tian blinds.

When I'm dead, throw a gun on the casket, he said
to no one.

The Path

Perhaps I'll live
forever in my physical body.

But if not, when I go,
words
may be all
that
remain behind.

Like bread crumbs,
dropped
along the way.

The Dog Did It

Tomorrow,
we shall try this dance
just one more time.

All worn out now;
it's the end of the day.

And like a hound dog,
plopping itself down
onto a dusty wooden porch at twilight,
sneaking one last gaze at the horizon,

then drifting into a little nap
with a sigh,
and passing a bit of gas,

this day passes
from today
into yesterday.

Father Luke

Something Other Than Myself

A sheriff is diverting traffic.

A mother bear is trying
to drag her dead cub off the highway.

Nothing is more important to me now
than slowing to a stop, and allowing another
their grief.

We are, all of us,
so alone.

Hosho McCreesh

Hosho McCreesh

In Every Place The Sun Drags It's Light,
& In Every Shadow That Aches For It,
In Every Single Place That Exists,
& In Every Single Place We Can Imagine...

...the irrefutable, undeniable
truth
is that
despite maybe
wanting to,
we
cannot
do it all
alone,
our humanity
prevents
it—

for the
better
I think.

In This Our Darkest Night,
In This Our Age Of Stillness,
Of No Light, No Insight, No Inertia...

...we've allowed
our inner machinations
to convince us of
so
much
madness
that we now have to
struggle
to even turn
our faces
to the
sun

&

smile.

Hosho McCreesh

October in America

It was a time of spiders & thieves,
that was where we were forced
to make our stand.

The newsmen just trolled on by,
reported what they were told to report,
then ordered fried shrimp sandwiches
& chewed with their mouths open.

Nights were spent alone,
millions & millions of people alone.

There were fires, wars, protests
organized by schemers, pundits, & shills,
while old men sat reading the paper,
wishing they could still smoke.

Too many dead birds,
too many chained dogs,
too many needing
something safe to rely on,
it made most of us do
desperate things.

Tiny cracks appeared in the structures
& there just wasn't much innocence left.

People tried to fuck each other
without risking anything else,

& most everyone tried to think of
things to sell while their
sons & daughters & husbands & wives
were being martyred out there in the
gypsum & sun-bleached sandstorms.

The poor & the rich drank too much,
heckled the rest of us from their
golden porches or piss-stained alleys.

It was clear that none of us would survive.

It was October in America
& it was all more terrible
than anyone was
willing to
admit.

Hosho McCreesh

They're Feeding The Pigeons In Venice, & Someone In Amsterdam, In Paris, Is Standing In Front Of A van Gogh Weeping...

...because they understand it,
understand that there's just
not much
grace
left,
understand that almost everywhere there is an
inescapable ugliness
& that the soul grows tired of its shell,
of being told not to scream
when all it wants to do is
sing,
sing of this
miraculous
frail
misfit
that surrounds it, this
miraculous
frail
misfit
that stumbles through
hours & decades & drunken midnights,
loveless, wallowing, begging condolence like
scuffed pennies.

We should be sick of desperation,

sick of stagnation & lifelessness, joylessness,
sick of all that are content to be left
to this plague & pitter, content to just
dangle about like
spiders & cheap
earrings.

Amidst all we push around & carry,
all we imagine & invent,
all we kill ourselves to garner,
this
remains
the
only
crux:

There, once again,
begins the
snow—

—though the
clean
living
through
is
all.

Hosho McCreesh

A Poem For
Anyone
Who Cannot
Be
Happy...

Listen, we already know
how it
ends—

     ash & bone & dank, heavy soil

—the only thing we
don't
know
is

everything

in between.

**You Never Want To Say That
We Owe It To Ourselves
To Be As Happy As We Can Possibly Be
For All The Many & Nefarious Ways It'll Be
Taken Out Of Context, Be Co-Opted
By The Greedy, The Self-Important,
The Gluttonous, & Idiotic & Insatiable...**

...but we
do.

The giggling
skull
fidgets
under our
tired faces
waiting
patiently
for it's day,
the day it will
claw forth from within,
the day it will finally
laugh with
unchecked
abandon
at all our
useless
toil,
the day it will
drag out from
under all our

Hosho McCreesh

ridiculous
notions
& out into the
smoldering
sunshine...

...&, until then,
we owe it
to ourselves
to be as
happy
as we
can
be.

One For The People Who Think It's Easy To Write Poems, & For Those Who Think Poems About Ex-Lovers Actually Matter...

Heard a story once about a guy, a hiker,
who was attacked by something wild,
whatever it was gored & eviscerated him
& he literally had to drag his guts,
miles away, through the woods
to a road where he
collapsed.

A pair of headlights
would find him later,
& in the emergency room
they couldn't sedate him, they said,
he was too weak to survive it,
chances were they couldn't revive him if they did,
so they had to hand-wash his dangling intestines,
all kinked-up-raveled like a garden hose,
scrub away the
pebbles
grit
twigs &
pine needles
him wide awake, watching,
& feeling it all
full-bore, &
straight on
through...

Hosho McCreesh

He lived.

Now that's a
goddamned
poem.

As Madness Abounds, As Brutality Trumpets, & A Cold, Hard World Gets Colder, Harder, & The Death Of All That Might Save Us Increases...

...perhaps the
hardest part is to
continually
look
around &
know,
not think,
KNOW
that
this is not
how the
world
is
supposed
to
be.

One for the Bulls,
No, One for Us...

The waters off Spain
churn & spit,
all turbulence & tumult,
they amble, jibe,
buckle & crush
against battered, swollen banks
& we are mariners with
snapped oars, with
scurvy—
only fear and guts
remain.

Indeed we're born into this,
bred for it,
taught to accept it,
indoctrinated to willingly partake...

It's as natural as the bulls
bleeding into the Spanish earth,
everyone cheers
while the dust plumes rise
from blood-spattered, face-down nostrils,
like Lorca in Granada
we leak,
everything
just
seeps
out...

They need their
victories—
the have-nots must be
lynched
by the haves.
They need to sever the ear,
hold it high, & hail it,
as proud as any
crucifixion,
aloft & drip-dangling
for the
roar
of the
crowd.

Imagine all the
senseless spilt blood,
the centuries of bloodshed
draining into the center of the earth like a
rusted raingutter,
it's molten core crusted & caked,
scabbed over with it—
picture that & tell me
there's a
point &
purpose
to it
all.

There isn't.

Hosho McCreesh

Just as the yellowed-dry leaves of
graveyard trees
have never known
anything
but drunken tears &
sorrow...

We will never
win.

Not like they win.

We simply don't
need
it.

A Majestic 50 Year Old Cottonwood
Sick With Some Kind Of Infestation & Rot...

10 years ago
a girlfriend & I
were driving back home
arguing about
who knows what
when we happened on
a team of men
cutting down
a majestic 50 year old cottonwood
sick with some kind of infestation & rot.

The gnash & grrrrrr of the
chainsaws
built to an infuriating roar
as we passed silently,
the fighting no longer
as important.

She started crying
for the tree.

It was apropos of everything
& we said little else
& eventually ended.

A little drunk, a little tired,
a long, lonely decade in between,
it's one of the only things about her

that I still remember,
& the only thing
about her
that I

still

love.

Bios

Miles J. Bell was delivered to the wrong address in 1971 by a myopic, alcoholic and slightly amused stork that should have dropped him off somewhere more royal. His father was a boxer; his mother was a cocker spaniel. He lives and loves in England, with the world's only beautiful math teacher and two bipedal noise generators. When not writing poetry he is not a poet, and does other things. This doesn't mean he isn't still watching, amused and appalled, always.

MK Chavez writes about the beauty that can be found in ugliness. She has three chapbooks *Virgin Eyes*, (Zeitgeist Press) and *Visitation*, and *Next Exit #9* with john sweet (Kendra Special Editions.) You can find out about her up coming publications at www.littlebrownsparrow.com

Christopher Cunningham lives with his lady and his dogs in various reclusive states at a variety of undisclosed locations. He's published some books of poetry and letters, the latest of which are *A Sound To Drive Away The Coming Darkness* (Propaganda Press, 2008) and the forthcoming *Sunlight At Midnight, Darkness At Noon: The Cunningham/McCreesh Letters, 2002* (Orange Alert Press, 2009). Find him at http://savageheavens.blogspot.com

Father Luke waits with the woman he loves for a perfect world. You may find him at http://FatherLuke.com

Hosho McCreesh hails from the vast gypsum and caliche deserts of the American Southwest. He maintains his sanity by writing, painting, and loving Ms. Babineaux. Recent books are available from *Bottle of Smoke Press, Sunnyoutside* and *Orange Alert Press*; broadsides available via *Sore Dove Press* and *10pt Press*. Additional information and occasional updates can be found at: www.nyqpoets.net/poet/hoshomccreesh

Christopher Robin is a small publisher, laborer, and traveler from Santa Cruz, CA. In 1999 his friend published his first chapbook for him: *Who Will Pay the Royalties for the Voices in My Head?* His other chapbooks include *Freaky Mumbler's Manifesto* and the most recent, *Angelflies In My IdiotSoup* published by Platonic3Way Press. He has published Zen Baby zine, a pseudo literary train-wreck in print form, since the year 2000. His other interests include swap meets, gambling, coffee, and adult swim cartoons.

William Taylor Jr. lives in San Francisco with his wife and a cat named Trouble. His work has been widely published in the independent press and across cyberspace in such publications as *Poesy, Anthills* and *The New York Quarterly.* His poetry has twice been nominated for a Pushcart prize. *The Hunger Season*, a book of new poems, is due from Sunnyoutside in Fall 2009. His previous books include *So Much is Burning* (Sunnyoutside, 2006) and *Words For Songs Never Written: New and Collected Poems* (Centennial Press, 2007).

ABOUT THE LUMMOX PRESS

Lummox Press was created in 1994 by RD Armstrong. It began as a self-publishing/DIY imprint for poetry by RD. Several chapbooks were published and in late 1995 it began publishing the **Lummox Journal**, a monthly small/underground press lit-arts zine. Available primarily by subscription, the LJ continued it's exploration of the "creative process" until its demise as a print mag in 2006.

During its eleven year existence, this tiny mag with the big name, interviewed poets, musicians and artists (over 100 in all) about how they do what they do. Hundreds of poems were also published in its pages. Poets like *Todd Moore, Lyn Lifshin, Gerald Locklin, Holly Prado, L.A. Bogen, Linda Lerner, Scott Wannberg, Philomene Long, John Thomas* and *RD Armstrong,* to name a few, appeared regularly within its pages. It was hailed as one of the best monthly's in the small press.

In 1998, Lummox began publishing the **Little Red Book** series, and continues to do so today. To date there are some 63 titles in the series (as of 2009) and this year a collection of poems from the first decade of the series has been published under the title, **The Long Way Home** (2009).

Lummox also publishes limited edition books such as **The Wren Notebook** by Rick Smith (2000) and **Last Call: The Legacy of Charles Bukowski** (2004). More recently, Lummox published a set of four titles from its founder, RD Armstrong: **On/Off the Beaten Path** (a trio of long poems about road trips taken in 1999, 2000 and 2001 including the epic poem **RoadKill** – which John Berbrich said was "the best post 9-11 writing I've seen"), **Fire and Rain – Selected Poems 1993-2007** Volumes 1 & 2 and **El Pagano and Other Twisted Tales** (a collection of short stories and flash fiction). All were published in 2008. In late 2008 Lummox began publishing the *RESPECT* series starting with *John Yamrus'* **New and Selected Poems.** This was followed by *Todd Moore's* **The Riddle of the Wooden Gun** (2009); **Sea Trails** by *Pris Campbell* (2009) and **Down This Crooked Road – Modern Poetry from the Road Less Traveled** edited by *RD Armstrong and William Taylor, Jr.* (2009). These books are available directly from the Lummox Press via the website: www.lummoxpress.com or at **Lummox** c/o PO Box 5301 San Pedro, CA 90733. There are also E-Book versions of most titles available. The RESPECT series, as well as, RD's four titles are also available at Amazon.com.

Please visit the website to read selections from these titles as well as peruse the many other titles/articles published by the Lummox Press.

Ask your independent bookstore to carry these titles, since Lummox only deals with independent book stores like Powell's of Portland, OR; The Book Collector of Sacramento, CA or Moe's of Berkeley, CA.

Together with Chris Yeseta (Layout and Art Direction since 1997), RD continues to publish books that are both striking in their looks as well as their content…you'd think he was aping Black Sparrow, but he is merely trying to produce the best books he can for his clients, the poets, and their customers, you, the readers.

* * *

ABOUT RAINDOG

RD Armstrong (Raindog to his friends) lives in Long Beach, CA and plies his trade as a HANDYMAN & journeyman POET all over the Southern California area.

RD has been writing and actively participating in the poetry "scene" in the Los Angeles area for fifteen years. During his travels, he has met and befriended many Small Press poets, and can count among these both the famous and infamous. He divides his time between operating the Lummox Press, publishing the Little Red Book & the new RESPECT series, writing and working on the houses of his customers. What started out as his avocation, writing poetry and fiction, has now taken a back seat to his obligations as a small press mogul! Poetry has become a closeted obsession.

ABOUT THE NAME RAINDOG – it comes from a song/album by Tom Waits. It describes a dog that has lost his way in this crazy world.

CONTACT:
poetraindog@gmail.com
www.lummoxpress.com

www.ingramcontent.com/pod-product-compliance
Lightning Source LLC
Chambersburg PA
CBHW051841090426
42736CB00011B/1914

* 9 7 8 1 9 2 9 8 7 8 0 3 1 *